Why and How I Became a Zen Buddhist

From the Search

to Putting Zen into Practice

~ Will Snebold

Acknowledgements

I am eternally grateful to all my loved ones for their continuing support, as I pursue my heart of heart's passion for not only exploring and learning about Zen Buddhism, but also applying the Dharma (Buddhist teachings) to the practical side of my life; my actually putting Zen Buddhism into practice – and heretofore it being a life-long journey, worth every moment of it.

In particular, I wish to thank the following for their supportive role and morale-boosting efforts as I wrote this book: Neal Snebold, Susan Abbattista, Anacaite Caperton, Jonas Shelton, David Snebold, Laura Snebold, Stu McIntire, Jake Siegel, Steve Shelton, and Trent Robertson.

Thank you, one and all.

Contents

Introduction

1. Introducing Zen Buddhism. 1

2. From the Search. 6

3. To Putting Zen Theory-Therapy into Practice . .10

Part I

Why? – What Caught My Eye:

Three Intriguing Facets of Zen Buddhism

4. Three Intriguing Facets of Zen Buddhism: Unitive Experience, Impermanence, and 'Don't Know' Mind. 13

   a) Unitive Experience – Mind and Body Unite. 13

   b) Impermanence. 16

   c) 'Don't Know' Mind. 19

5. Zen's Iconoclastic, Radical Approach. 24

Part II

Why? – My 25 Years of Practicing a Variation of Gufu-Shogyo-Zen, Avoiding Sitting Meditation

6. What Gufu-Shogyo-Zen is: 'Fool's Zen'. 28

7. Why That Only and Not Zazen (Sitting Meditation) for All These Years? What Was I Afraid Of?. 31

Part III

How? – Arriving at Practicing Zen

8. Zazon, Analytical Meditation, and Focusing. . . 38

a) Zazen. 38

b) Analytical Meditation. 40

c) Focusing. 44

9. It Can Take the Place of Prayer in My Zen Practice. 47

Part IV

How? – Practice of Unitive Experience,

Impermanence,

and 'Don't Know' Mind

10. Zen: It's Similar to What Zen monk Qingyuan Weixin, Poet Wallace Stevens, and 1960s Folk Musician Donovan Describe. 54

Part V

How? – Philosophical Journey
into Zen Buddhism

11. Philosophical Journey, in Depth. 57

Part VI (Section 1)

How? – Psychological Journey
into Zen Buddhism

12. Delving into the Psychotherapeutic Aspects of Zen Meditation for Me. 69

Part VI (Section 2)

How? – Psychological Journey

into Zen Buddhism

13. Psychological Journey, Exegesis in Depth. . .92

Conclusion 140

Introduction

Note: All text citations throughout this work are in parentheses ( ).

1. Introducing Zen Buddhism

Zen (Chinese, Ch'an) literally means "meditation," or as The Dalai Lama sometimes speaks of it, "meditative stabilization." Zen is presented as being neither a religion, a psychology, nor a philosophy. And yet, there is something highly philosophical and psychological about Zen; something inquisitive, provocative, titillating, and alluring that is standing alongside it; sutras (Buddhist teachings) and koans (baffling mental puzzles) being clear examples.

Zen has nothing to do with some kind of religious, supernatural spookiness; no god/desses to worship; no savior or guru to save you; just a direction, a path that

1

lays bare the pure, naked experience of bare awareness of 'what is.' There is "no ultimate rescuer" (recalling psychoanalyst Irvin Yalom's *Existential Psychotherapy*). Rather, Zen fosters a single-pointed concentration, a mindfulness that taps into the bareness of existence, life's purest qualities.

Zen can be described as a form of cultivating an awareness of 'what is,' as opposed to projecting and superimposing dichotomous, subject/object, observer/observed notions and feelings upon reality, being entrapped by an Aristotelian logic, with its discriminating mind. In Zen, however, it is a matter of cultivating a 'non-discriminating mind' toward life.

What caught my eye regarding Zen Buddhism was the unitive, non-dualistic view of existence; where there is no mind/body dichotomy, no observer/observed duality, after all. For decades, I have yearned to experience a united my mind and body; to awaken to the fact that I and the universe are one whole thing, dependent arising, interdependency, as opposed to a dichotomous view of life. I'm here reminded of a line from "Persona" by film director Ingmar Bergman: "Why don't my actions tally with my thoughts?" This is the core of my 'problematic' throughout life. So, Zen comes along in my life 25 years ago to introduce me to a unitive way of viewing reality; a reality of non-duality. This is the core of what caught my eye about a Zen way of perceiving.

In Trevor Leggett's work, *A First Zen Reader,* he holds out – to my mind – the prospect of a united mind/body experience. He writes,

> The [Buddha] simply wished to show all living beings how to set in right order the body and mind. The method of doing this is given in the classic on meditation called Zazen-gi: Think the unthinkable. How to think the unthinkable? Be without thoughts – this is the secret of Zen meditation; the control of body and mind . . . (34).

In Mark Epstein's work, *Thoughts without a Thinker:*
Psychotherapy from a Buddhist Perspective, he
speaks of a non-dual, unitive experience, wherein
there is, in actuality, no such thing as a "thinker," only
thoughts. Epstein writes,

> This emphasis on the lack of a particular,
> substantive agent is the most distinctive
> aspect of traditional Buddhist
> psychological thought; it is the realization
> that transforms the experience of the
> Wheel of Life. But such a conception is
> not completely outside the realm of
> psychoanalysis. True thoughts "require
> no thinker," the psychoanalyst W.R. Bion
> echoed. . . . It is in this idea of "thoughts
> without a thinker" that psychoanalysis
> has approached the Buddhist view, for it
> is the elimination of narcissism that Bion
> is suggesting, a possibility that Buddhism
> also holds dear (41).

And,

For the self, according to the Buddha's language of the ancient Sutras, is a fiction – a mirage, a shadow, or a dream. In today's psychodynamic language, we would call it a fantasy, a pretense, or a wish (87).

2. From the Search

By way of studying Western philosophy, philosophy of religion (East and West), existentialism, phenomenology, postmodernism, metamodernism (post-post-modernism), psychology, poetry, aesthetics, including numerous years of studying Zen psychology and philosophy, and many Zen classics, sutras, precepts, and the such, I have Searched far and wide for a lifetime. I have garnered much from my studies. Yet, so finitely limited (by language and historicity) in grasping some sort of metaphysical comfort for myself. I have roller-coasted along all of these paths; sometimes hot, sometimes cold, but always in earnest throughout the Search. Search(es), rather. That is to say, I see existence through a prism; Nietzsche's perspectivism, Wallace Stevens' "13 Ways to Look at a Blackbird," phenomenology's layered examinations into the human experience.

I accept that the Search is with us always, and that's kind of cool, though sometimes cruel. Literary author writer Walker Percy submits for our approval:

6

The search is what anyone would undertake if he were not sunk in the everydayness of his own life. To become aware of the possibility of the search is to be onto something. Not to be onto something is to be in despair.

(Goodreads-Quotes).

Yes, not to be "onto something" is truly to be in despair; or even dis-repair. The Search(es), for me, have entailed some richly variegated fields of study, as referenced above. I have had a long-standing affinity for the wide net of hermeneutics (theories of interpretation), which takes in myriad ways in which to see and explain existence, especially human existence. In turn, I have been impacted by the way I see life: ethically, epistemologically, and ontologically: ethically, which has to do with value judgements; epistemologically, which deals in theories of knowledge, how we come to know; and ontologically, which attends to theories of metaphysics, for lack of better, more complicated terms.

Now, one necessarily starts where one is, without any kind of 20-20 hindsight as one's guide; without any metaphysical crystal ball. We have to make decisions and commit to actions – sometimes snap, other times gradual – that positively or negatively impact the universe around us; the myriad universes of discourse and discourses, to put it another way. We are forced, by 'nature,' to make decisions and commit to actions with ethical (recalling phenomenologist philosopher Emmanuel Levinas's stressing that "ethics is first philosophy") and karmic (to recall Buddhistic teachings) ramifications. On a deeper level, yes, the Search continues, but, by the same token, one must also make a stand with an ethical resolve of some sort, a resolute constitution in life. I must make an ethical stand, however limited my epistemological or ontological understanding may be; separating (what I happen to deem) the wheat from the chaff as to what informs and constitutes me, provisionally speaking of course.

Life's choices sometimes seem like an affront to our senses, other times gentler nudging; it's a lot like a whirlwind of activity that preoccupies our minds, constantly, 24/7; sometimes subtly, other times severely so; with little to no relent. Ergo, each one of us should and, in fact, must make an "ethical" stand of some sort (Martin Buber and Levinas get all the credit for this heavy underscoring on my part).

My Search of a lifetime has been ensconced in philosophy proper, academe; my incessant use of terms couched, and even shrouded, in nebulosity. And for that, I must apologize to all my friends. Yet, for me, all my 'ten-dollar' words have served me as a kind of shorthand and set of abbreviations describing how and what I am. I like the pithiness of abbreviations, as it turns out. And that's one of the reasons why I like the language of poetry, for its pithiness. For that matter, this, too, is why I appreciate aesthetics/fine arts so much; "every picture tells a story, don't it?" (Rod Stewart sang it best). As the proverbial saying goes, "a picture is worth a thousand words."

3. To Putting Zen Theory-Therapy into Practice

Finally, from the 'Search' to a new-found faith and resolve in Zen Buddhism, discovering a self-reliance that gradually rules my life! I have finally begun awakening the Buddha nature, "enlightened one," within. I have always had that capacity, but it lay dormant for almost the entirety of my life. And, having spent numerous years reading and studying Zen Buddhist literature and Buddhistic principles, yet, not putting into practice zazen (sitting meditation) – so with no excuse – I have finally accepted and begun relying on my capacity to take control of my frame of mind and to own up to my responsibility to harness and utilize the power and crystal clarity of my own Buddhahood, my self-reliance with which to navigate through this world of ours; this world of 'maya' (illusion) and 'samsara' (the cycle of birth, death, and rebirth).

With the help of Zen Buddhism, I have become freer to practice the framing and reframing of my worldviews; to the point of feeling freer, in gradations of course, less incumbered with the weight of 'dukkha' (suffering). It is a freedom worth 'celebrating,' as opposed to 'cerebrating' (my former "Search" self); for, I haven't felt this good in a long, long time. Not that Zen is all about "feeling good," it's not; but as I am still a novice to practicing 'zazen' and analytical meditation, I can only report that I feel better and better about myself and the world-universe-universes-nothing around me. The best way I can put it is to say that I feel more integrated with life's 'rules of the road,' more accepting of the way life works; especially when it comes to life's dukkha (suffering) and obligatory death.

Putting Zen into practice, especially via zazen and analytical meditation, has deeply enriched my life thus far. These two forms of meditation have helped me immensely. (More on that later.) Putting Zen into practice, ever so briefly, I can now couple this to further use with my 25 years of "reading Zen," as I call it; some semblance of a form of meditation; not a 'sitting meditation' but a 'reading meditation,' as I like to call it. But it's one thing to study the precepts of Zen, and quite another to put these Zen principles into practice. I'm a work in progress.

My approach to 'meditating' on Buddhistic principles has, thus, shifted – in a very good way – toward meditatively exploring the 'experiential' realm of my newfound faith; integrating with a life that is much more philosophically robust and psychologically rewarding than merely 'reading Zen.'

Part I

Why? – What Caught My Eye:

Three Intriguing Facets of Zen Buddhism

4. Three Intriguing Facets of Zen Buddhism: Unitive Experience, Impermanence, and 'Don't Know' Mind

a) Unitive Experience – Mind and Body Unite

The prospect of viewing human existence as a unitive, mind-body unification, nondual in nature, greatly attracted me to the Zen Buddhist 'way of seeing.' In the pursuit of fathoming what Zen Buddhism has ascertained about life, that life is nondual and non-antagonistic, held out enormous beneficial results – philosophically, spiritually, and especially psychologically. For clarification of the Zen Buddhist notion of nonduality, consider this:

Nondualism in Mahayana Buddhism

Buddhism proposes that all phenomena inter-exist; nothing is separate. All phenomena are perpetually conditioning all other phenomena. Things are the way they are because everything else is the way it is.

Mahayana Buddhism teaches that these interdependent phenomena also are empty of self-essence or inherent characteristics. All distinctions we make between this and that are arbitrary and exist only in our thoughts. This doesn't mean that nothing exists, but that nothing exists the way we think it does.

If nothing is separate, how do we count the myriad phenomena? And does that mean everything is One? Mahayana Buddhism often comes across as a form of monism or the teaching that all phenomena are of one substance or are one phenomenon in principle. But Nagarjuna said that phenomena are neither one nor many. The correct answer to "how many?" is "not two."

The most pernicious dualism is that of the subjective "knower" and an object of knowing. Or, in other words, the perception of "me" and "everything else."

In the Vimalakirti Sutra, the layman Vimalakirti said that wisdom is "the elimination of egoism and possessiveness. What is the elimination of egoism and possessiveness? It is freedom from dualism. What is freedom from dualism? It is the absence of involvement with either the external or the internal. ... The internal subject and the external object are not perceived dualistically." When the dualism of subjective "knower" and object of "knowing" does not arise, what remains is a pure being or pure awareness.

(Nondualism in Mahayana Buddhism (learnreligions.com))

15

b) Impermanence

Another facet of Zen that I was extremely intrigued by was its notion of "impermanence;" for impermanence (anicca) deeply resonated with me, consciously and subconsciously, emotionally, and even somatically. Zen's 'way of seeing' underscored, to my mind and psyche, an important insight about existence; an impermanence that had a ring of truth about it, beginning for me many years ago. The Buddhist notion of anicca indicates   that life is transitoriness, constantly changing – never not – presenting life as precarious, contingent, unpredictable, uncertain, and fragile. Put another way, life and existence are non-inherently so; "empty," "nothing," sheer "void" (sunyata), lacking any inherently existent being. I hasten to add, sunyata is not to be misconstrued with the popularized Western notion of nihilistic nothingness; not that kind of denigrating, destructive void of futile meaninglessness.

Why was this so important to me, I ask myself? My best guess – actually it's palpably clear to me – is that my dad's premature death at age 44, while I was age

12, left an indelible mark on my psyche. I was deeply hurt.

There were a few other factors going on back then in my psyche. Suffice it to say, I had become deeply disturbed by the seeming finality of death and impermanence; a certain feeling of anticipatory dread set in – what I have since called my "dead dread" – owing to the fact that my psyche was indelibly marked, fragmented, and distorted; all leaving me with a forever (I exaggerate) untrusting sense of the world around me, that the world is diabolical and not to be trusted. Such an ugly 'way of seeing.')

I became infatuated with this Zen vision of life being impermanence. It took numerous years of merely reading and studying Zen Buddhist literature, especially Buddhist psychology, before I would truly embrace it. I was on a novice level of appreciating Buddhism, intellectual solely. My practice (if I even had one) would consider what I was doing a form of "reading Zen," in lieu of any real meditation – such as "sitting Zen" or "walking Zen." It took forever to actually begin to truly value (partially, anyway) and apply "impermanence" to life's situations, however dire and dreadful the 'news of bad news' might present itself.

Impermanence and transitoriness, I have come to learn, is not all scary. According to Zen Buddhist Thich Nhat Hanh,

> Understanding impermanence can give us confidence, peace, and joy. Impermanence does not necessarily lead to suffering. . . . We need to learn to appreciate the value of impermanence. If we are in good health and are aware of impermanence, we will take good care of ourselves. When we know that the person we love is impermanent, we will cherish our beloved all the more. Impermanence teaches us to respect and value every moment and all the precious things around us and inside of us. When we practice mindfulness of impermanence, we become fresher and more loving.

(The Heart of the Buddha's Teaching, 132)

c) 'Don't Know' Mind

According to the quite popular, contemporary Buddhist teacher and author, Jack Kornfield,

> Use this practice ['don't know' mind] to bring wisdom to a situation of inner or outer conflict. Initially begin by sitting. Later you can practice in social situations.
>
> Sit quietly and easily, focusing on your breath or body. When you feel settled, bring to mind a time ten years ahead. Recognize that you don't know what will happen then. Feel the not knowing and

relax with it. Think of the earth spinning through space with hundreds of thousands of people being born and dying every day. Where does each life come from? How did it start? There are so many things we don't know. Feel the truth of don't know mind, relax and become comfortable with it.

Now, bring to mind a conflict, inner or outer. Be aware of all the thoughts and opinions you have about how it should be, about how they should be. Now recognize that you don't really know. Maybe the wrong thing will lead to something better. You don't know.

Consider how would it be to approach yourself, the situation, the other people with don't know mind. Feel it. Don't know. Not sure. No fixed opinion. Allow yourself to want to understand anew. Approach it with don't know mind. With openness. How does don't know mind affect the situation? Does it improve it, make it wiser, easier? More relaxed?

Practice don't know mind until you are comfortable resting in uncertainty, until you can do your best and laugh and say "Don't know."

(Practice: Don't Know Mind (jackkornfield.com), 2015)

This, the third facet of Zen Buddhism, that captured my attention was its emphasis on and sanctioning of a humble admittance that we Homo sapiens just don't know, even though we like to think that we do. We hold on to this or that epistemological paradigm (theory of knowledge, how we know) in order to establish a confidence – bordering on hubris – that absolutizes our particular set of opinions about the ultimate meaning of life, mystery solved. But, in point of fact, we are all living our lives with a false sense of security here. However much our scientific, empirical grasp of 'facts' becomes, our "human, all too human" (echoing Nietzsche) understanding of life – the big picture – nevertheless remains partial and incomplete. We Homo sapiens remain in the dark; the more we know, the more we don't know (recall Socrates). It's always been this way, throughout human history, without exception. And, so shall it remain this way, owing to the condition of being human, operating with our all too human, finite and feeble understanding, our limited tools of linguisticality. As the biblical verse reminds us, "for now we see through a glass darkly."

To cope with this human predicament, Zen Buddhism offers tools and practices, such as the humble admittance of the 'don't know' mind, in order to put human knowledge into perspective; finite and historical, limited and provisional. The Buddhist tool of putting the 'don't know' mind into a practice enables one to live and cope with the human condition that there are no absolutes to be had in life. However tempted we are to absolutize our opinions about life, informed or not, there is no escape from the human condition of limited knowing.

Practicing 'don't know' mind helps to put all of life into perspective, striking a chord of balance, equanimity, and humility.

5. Zen's Iconoclastic, Radical Approach

Zen Buddhism also struck a chord with me in its radical bursting the bubble of hubris and humankind's tendencies towards an absolutizing disposition. Zen appealed to me for its iconoclastic and radical way of treating the human condition, underscoring the limitations of language. This is exampled in the following citations:

> An ancient Zen master, Ummon, when asked what is Buddha, replied, "shit on a stick."

And,

> *A monk asked Ummon, "What is Buddha?"*
> *Ummon replied, "Kanshiketsu!"*
> Kanshiketsu, literally is "shit stick"."

Take the case of Zen koans, paradoxes, and logical puzzles; all with the purpose of liberating the recipient from being stuck in in their discriminating, dualistic, Aristotelian, Cartesian mind; mired in fractionized thinking and way of seeing life.

Yet another ancient Zen master, Lin-chi, once put it this way,

> "If you meet the Buddha, kill him."

Modern day psychoanalyst Sheldon Kopp would incorporate this wild statement into the title of his book, "If You Meet the Buddha on the Road, Kill Him!"

I cite these examples in order to exemplify the iconoclastic and radical aspects of the Zen way of being, the Zen way of thinking, the Zen way of seeing, the Zen way of grasping our "human, all too human" linguistical medium.

Now, 'the Beats' – the Beat poets of the 50s and 60s, such as Jack Kerouac, Allen Ginsberg, Lawrence Ferlinghetti, and Gary Snyder – took radical approaches by applying Zen, with poetic license, in order to shatter the dualistic, linear, pedestrian ways of thinking and looking at life.

The part-zennist author Alan Watts does not always see eye to eye with "the Beats" way of approaching Zen. In his book "This Is It," Watts devotes a whole chapter to the 'Beats' and their misappropriations – or, at least, taking too far – the message of Zen. Watts suggests,

> When Kerouac gives his philosophical final statement, "I don't know. I don't care. And it doesn't make any difference" – the cat is out of the bag, for there is a hostility in these words which clangs with self-defense. But just because Zen truly

surpasses convention and its values, it has no need to say 'To hell with it,' nor to underline with violence the fact that anything goes. (Alan Watts, *This Is It*, p. 92).

D.T. Suzuki and Shunryu Suzuki – two pioneering zennists, who built bridges between the East and the West – were primed for introducing the iconoclastic radicalness of the Zen way of seeing. Full of foreign (in the Westerners eyes) concepts from the East made major breakthroughs in transforming the mindset of countless human beings in the West.

Part II

Why? – My 25 Years Practicing a Variation of

Gufu-Shogyo-Zen, Avoiding Sitting Meditation

6. What Gufu-Shogyo-Zen is: 'Fool's Zen'

A brief introduction to my 25 years of sloppily, partially practicing, unbeknownst to me, a form of Zen meditation, is in order. About 10 years ago, I discovered that there was such a thing as the gufu-shogy-zen tradition:

> If you are sitting around thinking about impermanence, this is "gufu-shogyo-zen" or "fool's zen."
>
> Stainless | White Wind Zen Community (wwzc.org)

Gufu-shogyo-zen is, to my understanding, a novice-level, introductory phase in practicing Zen meditation by studying and meditating on Zen Buddhist precepts;

28

principles, such as impermanence (anicca), emptiness (mu), dependent arising-interdependency (sunyata), and "don't know" mind. *The Encyclopedia of Eastern Philosophy and Religion*, eds., Stephan Schuhmacher and Gert Woerner, states:

> Gufu-shogyo-zen: Jap., literally "fools zen;" Zen expression for the style of meditation in which one thinks about orthodox doctrinal ideas (for example, impermanence, egolessness, emptiness, etc.). Zen distinguishes true Zen practice (zazen) from this conventional style of meditation, ruling out preoccupation with religious notions, however holy they may be, in order to free the mind from dependence on thinking.

There is very little mention of this form of meditation in my research. But it makes sense to me, and especially to prioritize the varying forms of meditation. I think I can put gufu-shogyo-zen meditation in the proper frame of mind; it has its place, but one should not be consumed or preoccupied with cogitating solely.

Given my propensity for philosophizing most of my life, such cerebrating will always be with me, but in a more 'positive' light, with the awareness of, and meditation on, Zen's notion of Buddha nature to accompany me "through a glass darkly."

'Fools zen. But all to the neglect of a more promising form of meditation – zazen (sitting meditation). I have now been practicing zazen with a friend for about two years, and I never looked back, so to speak. Actually, I've had a few reservations; only in that I felt myself gradually loosening my grip on 'philosophy proper' (with its philosophical jargon), which, of course, has its place, too. Maybe just not at this time in my life.

7. Why That Only and Not Zazen (Sitting Meditation) for All These Years? What Was I Afraid Of?

> I have my books and my poetry to protect
> me. I am shielded in my armor. Hiding in
> my room, safe within my womb. I touch
> no one and no one touches me. I am a
> rock, I am an island. And a rock feels no
> pain, and an island never cries.
>
> (Simon and Garfunkel, I Am A Rock)

Reluctance number one:

This stanza expresses my guide and 'guard' almost my entire life. Through a process of misinterpreting the song – thinking it was valorizing these lines – I misunderstood it to be a legitimate way I could psychologically defend myself against the harsh onslaughts that life naturally presents.

I've been hiding within my studies of philosophy, religion, and Zen psychology, in part at least, because of my fear of people's "words" that have the potential to hurt me. I have morphed in terms of the ways I've accomplished this feat, this feet of clay. Of course, I rationalized that it was in order to keep an open mind to everything; having cultivated a kind of 'checks and balances' to ward off the temptation of fanaticism, extremism, diving off the deep end, on my part. For decades, I've sworn to myself that I would never get duped again, never get caught off guard by religion; all religions that perilously preach some sort of spooky supernaturalism that must be bowed down to and worshipped. I wanted no part of it. "Fool me once, shame on you. Fool me twice, shame on me."

The core of my reluctance, and even outright conscious resistance, toward meditation has been borne out of a deep-seated fear of getting hurt, yet again, by my fanatical tendencies. The first time being, I let myself go headlong into earnest prayer and praying during the numerous years of my 'falling for' the evangelical, bible-thumping, hyper-Calvinist brand of "born again" Christianity, hook, line, and sinker; what Eric Hoffer refers to as a "true believer." I was a fanatical, absolutist kind of believer for a very long time.

But, after numerous years of fervent prayer and trust, believing in Jesus as my Lord and Savior (what existential psychoanalyst Irvin Yalom refers to as some people's need for an "ultimate rescuer"), I 'fell from grace' by asking too many questions; questions that remained unanswered, raising my doubts exponentially with every course I took in Western philosophy. The Elders of the church practically 'excommunicated' me for my operating on the basis of "honest answers to honest questions," as one evangelical apologist put it. Getting my degree in Philosophy was the 'penultimate' stage of freeing myself from the bondage of absolutist thinking and religious fanaticism. It is to philosophy's credit that I was able to rid myself of my religious narrow-mindedness, incrementally, over the years.

My partial Buddha awakenings via Gufu-shogyo-zen – my mini-enlightenments, so to speak (or some semblance of brief kenshos) – have come along with my studies, and partial practice, of Zen. Unbeknownst to me, over the numerous years of studying and reading Zen – yet never actually meditating till recently

– I realize now two things: one, that as the Zen masters would frequently say of anyone in my position, I "stink of Zen," meaning I indulge myself in reading and studying the dharma; Zen teachings, precepts, tenets, such as anicca (impermanence), sunyata (emptiness, nothing) tathata (the suchness and thusness), mu (empty), dependent arising, karma, Nirvana, etc.) and thinking and dwelling on their meaning, in terms of Zen's principles of life; and two, that my voracious reading of Zen literature was some form of a 'practice,' a practice known from the Gufu-shogyo-zen tradition as 'fool's zen;' a tradition whereby the practitioner does not practice zazen (sitting meditation), but rather studies and meditates on Zen precepts; tenets that run lofty and deep, being highly abstract, paradoxical, philosophical, psychological, and spiritual in nature. But even so, Zen makes no claim that Buddhism is a philosophy, psychology, or religion.

Reluctance number two:

My aversion to meditation was also owing to my preoccupation with philosophical concerns. My studies of postmodernism over the years left me believing that there was no such thing as a pure, unmediated, unadulterated experience of life. That is to say, the postmodernist perspective of linguisticality views language as intermediary, not direct; language is a necessary conduit, the medium through which hermeneutical bridge-building attempts to understand experience. For the postmodernist, there is no such thing as a pure, direct experience. Life is always, never not, bridged by human language.

In a very important work – *The Problem of Pure Consciousness: Mysticism and Philosophy*, ed. Robert K.C. Forman – on this subject matter of whether there can ever be a "direct, first-hand experience" it is debated in detail by various essayists, weighing the pros and cons of the belief in a "pure consciousness event" (PCE), covering the full spectrum of beliefs and disbeliefs regarding the very possibility of a pure, unmediated experience, as reported by the mystics throughout history.

In this collection of essayists, 'to PCE or not to PCE' is the question. Can there be a pure, direct contact with the ineffable, the infinite, the god/desses; or, is it the case that human language always, never not, is the epistemological go-between for anything and everything? For the "constructivist," one can "never outrun conceptualization;" there is "no transcending language;" no pure event or experience." No PCE.

Constructivists, along with Steven Katz's "mystical constructivism," presume that,

> There are NO pure (i.e., unmediated) experiences. Neither mystical experience nor more ordinary forms of experience give any indication, or any grounds for believing, that they are unmediated. . . The notion of unmediated experience seems, if not self-contradictory, at best empty. This epistemological fact seems to me to be

true, because of the sorts of beings we are, even with regard to the experiences of those ultimate objects of concern with which mystics have had intercourse, e.g., God, Being, nirvana, etc.

(Found in Forman's "Introduction: Mysticism, Constructivism, and Forgetting," in *The Problem of Pure Consciousness: Mysticism and Philosophy*, p. 9; Katz excerpt taken from Katz's "Language, Epistemology, and Mysticism," in Katz's *Mysticism and Philosophical Analysis, p. 26*).

It's kind of like the proverbial distinction between just studying and talking about a body of water (its scientific properties, etc.) versus actually jumping in – ahh, that is true experiencing.

Part III

How? – Arriving at Practicing Zen

8. Zazen, Analytical Meditation, and Focusing

a) Zazen

First, zazen is "sitting meditation," sitting in silence while emptying the mind of thoughts, a process of allowing thoughts to just pass through without judgement, without examining the thoughts; a practice that my body and brain initially kicked and screamed about, until finally I am finding it to be richly rewarding to my head and my heart. A musical aside: "Jumping up and down the floor, my head is an animal . . ." – Of Monsters and Men.

Zazen has acted as an anchor – a space of solace and succor, emotionally and mentally – just by my observing my breath, in and out over and over. This practice entails the simple act of watching my breath and nothing else. In turn, it is an emptying of one's thoughts. Harder than it sounds, but I return to this practice in order to 'regulate' my mental and emotional streams of consciousness; to regulate the incessant mental activity of our "monkey mind;" to enforce (without too much force, of course) the habit regardless of how I feel on a given day. From my perspective, zazen begats equanimity, even-keeled composure and internal peace (most of the time, but not always; there are no guarantees).

b) Analytical Meditation:

Analytical meditation entails, in silence, meditatively examining mental activity, breaking down the troublesome thoughts – one thought per session – and truly processing what lies down deep that needs addressing, or, more importantly, needs self-transcending. The Dalai Lama fully subscribes to analytical meditation, referring to such meditation in several of his books. In a way, it strikes me as sort of like 'visualization' exercises that have become popular in the West. This exercise also strikes me as a lot like being in psychotherapy sessions; in this case, analytical meditation resemble self-psychotherapy, self-transcendingly so.

For the past two years, I've added another form of meditation to my life; something that The Dalai Lama refers to as "analytical meditation," whereby, instead of emptying thoughts, it meditatively engages one's mental activity.

It has taken me the better part of 25 years to finally realize my egregious neglect of – even obstinate fighting against – Zen meditation. But now, I have been practicing 'sitting meditation' (zazen) for two years, along with grafting "analytical meditation," as taught by The Dalai Lama in particular, and Eugene Gendlins' "focusing" techniques into the meditative process for the past year.

My aspiration to 'sit' and 'let it be' has led me to explore and partially experience – albeit a novice's level of fathoming – the essence, or some semblance thereof, of Zen awareness. "For now we see through a glass darkly." Though not normally highlighted in Zen literature, I think there is an 'apophatic' element in the Zen way of seeing. Apophatic comes from apophasis (Gk.), 'non-knowing,' 'knowing only in part,' 'knowing by negation, by what something is not,' what Western philosophers refer to as "Socratic ignorance," admitting that human knowing, in the ordinary sense, is always through a thinly veiled linguistical medium. For Zen, the apophatic element would be the awareness and practice of what is called "Great Doubt," acknowledging the "don't know" mind aspect of life's ambiguities, antinomies, and paradoxes. As echoed in the zennist tradition, 'If you have one conceptual thought, you are in error.' The mental level of activity must be partially suspended, bracketed, held provisionally, when it comes to human beings' knowledge and understanding of the world around us.

Fast forward to the present, I have discovered for the first time – on an experiential level – the reassuring message that comes to me by truly meditating on anicca, the 'impermanence' of the universe, of everything. There are, of course, numerous Zen precepts to meditate on, but sunyata is where I began with my meditation, having studied, in gufu-shogyo-zen fashion, the Zen principle of impermanence. Somehow, I gather solace and strength from such a contemplation. It takes the "sting out of death."

According to The Dalai Lama, there is no such thing as an autonomous, free-floating 'I,' no inherent existing 'I,' at least from an ultimate viewpoint. The 'I' we commonly and mistakenly speak of is, after all, not true ultimately. The 'I' exists only in conventional terms, conventional truths. The Dalai Lama uses a 'table' as an analogy for the bigger picture: A table is a table conventionally speaking, comprised of its parts (table top, legs, bolts, etc.). Dismantle the table to its relative parts, and where, then, is the 'table?' The table is nowhere to be found; rather, the table is a table, being comprised of multiple aggregates. So, what I take from The Dalai Lama's analogue is that there both is and is not a 'table,' speaking in conventional and ultimate perspectives respectively. By extrapolation, there both is and is not an 'I' to speak of.

In the past couple of years, I have learned about a form of meditation The Dalai Lama refers to as "analytical meditation," a form of meditation unlike zazen practice, zazen being a state of just letting mental activity float by like clouds in the sky. In analytical meditation, on the other hand, one dwells on and examines one's mental activity, analyzing it and just being with it, in order to achieve meditational stabilization. Analytical meditation appeals to me, perhaps because of my preoccupation with the discipline of philosophy in my background. This form of meditative stabilization can also meditate and examine any of the precepts or principles of Zen. Analytical meditation is, in many ways, not unlike a psychotherapy session. It is a form of catharsis for me, who happens to have a background in getting my head "shrunk" by psychotherapists over the decades, especially Dialectical Behavioral Therapy (DBT).

c) Focusing:

As an adjunct to practicing analytical meditation, my zazen friend and I have also relied on Eugene Gendlin's classic work, "Focusing," wherein his premise is that one can attune oneself to the "felt sense" and "shift" that takes place while in the process of focusing. For me, it's a way of framing and reframing my interpretive feelings towards life's situations that present themselves on a daily basis. He writes,

> A person's experience cannot be 'figured out' by others, or even by the person experiencing it. It cannot be expressed in

common labels. It has to be met, found, felt, attended to, and allowed to show itself. (156).

And,

A felt sense doesn't come to you in the form of thoughts or words or other separate units, but as a single . . . bodily feeling . . . It is [a] down-deep level of awareness (33).

And,

A felt sense is not an emotion like anger, fear, hate, joy, or anxiety. It is a sense of your total emotional situation (101).

"Focusing" is a part of analytical meditation. As well, "focusing" is a practice that philosopher Eugene Gendlin developed in his book, "Focusing," which describes in detail, breaking down the steps involved in such a technique. In my focusing sessions, a problem emotion is isolated and processed through stages of getting a handle on what ails one emotionally; then asking, how does this help me and how does this harm me; then, waiting for a somatic "shift," a space to "replace" my problem with a helping spirit or technique with which to maintain equanimity, self-composure.

9. It Can Take the Place of Prayer in My Zen Practice

Anecdotally speaking:

While practicing zazen and analytical meditation recently, I made a refreshing discovery that Zen meditation can, after a fashion, take the place of prayer, experientially speaking, for me. That is, in the god(dess)/less age I live – where there is no hocus-pocus, spooky supernaturalism – it dawns on me that Zen meditation can provide the same experience of elation, or bliss, as that of earnest praying back in my evangelical years.

Phenomenologically speaking:

If I had to make a phenomenological examination of my meditative experience, it would go like this: Eyes closed for 25 minutes (which is not a very long time), I began to feel myself observing myself. 'Observing myself observing.' But it didn't stop there, for I began to feel, in a very emotive fashion, myself stepping back from my 'self,' a suspension, a detachment from my conventional 'I.' 'I' was nowhere to be found. And it felt like a psychological/emotional buffer from 'myself,' from my physical and mental pains. It was the most serene 25-minute meditation that I have ever had, ever since my evangelical days of earnest prayer in my youth. And the elation/serenity lasted for an entire month.

Analytically speaking:

If Zen (meditation) is not a religion, psychology, or philosophy, then, how to proceed in analyzing my month-long experience of elation (or extreme serenity, at least)? One theory is that meditation "increases the brain's alpha waves," and that is all there is to it. I'm here referencing a Psychology Today article, which states:

> It's impossible for us to make our thoughts disappear; often, the more we

try to suppress them, the louder they become. But practicing meditation can help clear away the mind's chatter. Studies show that meditating even for as little as 10 minutes increases the brain's alpha waves (associated with relaxation) and decreases anxiety and depression. . . .

In mindfulness meditation, one turns their attention to a single point of reference, such as one's breath or bodily sensations, or a word or phrase known as a mantra. The practice has been shown to decrease distraction and rumination, make negative automatic thoughts seem easier to let go of, and promote greater enjoyment of the present moment. Loving-kindness meditation directs one's focus toward developing feelings of goodwill, kindness, and warmth for others. It can help boost empathy and compassion, and curb charged responses to negative thoughts.

(Meditation | Psychology Today)

Perhaps my month-long experience of bliss has a strictly neuro-scientific explanation, that meditation "increases the brain's alpha waves," according to the article below:

> Studies have shown that meditating regularly can help relieve symptoms in people who suffer from chronic pain, but the neural mechanisms underlying the relief were unclear. Now, MIT and Harvard researchers have found a possible explanation for this phenomenon.
>
> In a study published online April 21 in the journal *Brain Research Bulletin*, the researchers found that people trained to meditate over an 8-week period were better able to control a specific type of

brain waves called alpha rhythms.

"These activity patterns are thought to minimize distractions, to diminish the likelihood stimuli will grab your attention," says Christopher Moore an MIT neuroscientist [currently at Brown University] and senior author of the paper. "Our data indicate that meditation training makes you better at focusing, in part by allowing you to better regulate how things that arise will impact you."

(The benefits of meditation | MIT News | Massachusetts Institute of Technology)

I happen to subscribe to the corelative theory, one that does not conflict with the neuroscientific explanation; that what is experienced via meditation is a "unitive" bonding "awareness" that body and mind are one. This is the phenomenological 'take-away' that most impresses me, as making the most sense of what happened to me, to my psyche.

Much scientific research has been devoted to this phenomenon, for instance,

> Meditation can help increase awareness of the mind-body connection and provide both mental and physical health benefits. For example, mindfulness meditation and meditative relaxation techniques tie together calming of the mind with calming of the body. This allows for a holistic mind-body state of relaxation. Other meditation techniques and exercises, including deep breathing and progressive relaxation, can also help calm the mind and the body together and regulate the body's stress response.

> There is also evidence that meditation can cause changes to brain structures

that influence the physical body. Research suggests that meditation can result in changes to the anterior cingulate cortex and somatosensory cortex areas of the brain, which decreases pain sensitivity. Therefore its shown that meditation can positively impact pain levels. Research shows that meditative practice can result in changes to the Amyglada (fight or flight response), which can decrease the body's heart rate and blood pressure.

Learn How Meditation and The Mind Body Connection Works (anahana.com)

As good working hypotheses, both the neuroscientific research results and the Buddhistic explanation of the meditative experience – awareness of the unitive mind-body reality – are satisfactory hypotheses that do not conflict with one another.

Part IV

How? – Practice of Unitive Experience, Impermanence, and 'Don't Know' Mind

10. Zen: It's Similar to What Zen monk Qingyuan Weixin, Poet Wallace Stevens, and 1960s Folk Musician Donovan Describe

> "First there is a mountain, then there is no mountain, then there is."
>
> (Donovan, There is a Mountain, off his Greatest Hits album).

This song is clearly a nod to Zen monk Qingyuan Weixin, who spoke thus:

> Before a man studies Zen to him mountains are mountains and waters are

waters; after he gets an insight into the truth of Zen through the instruction of a good master, mountains to him are not mountains and waters are not waters; but after this when he really attains to the abode of rest, mountains are once more mountains and waters are waters.

Mountains . . .

No Mountains . . .

Mountains again . . .

Quite a provocative way of seeing (or interpreting) life, 'what is.' It is an interesting phenomenological approach to better ascertaining the details of these three variant experiences.

Mountains – The beginner's (uninitiated) perspective: Before Zen meditation, mountains are merely mountains, taken for granted, without truly appreciating the nigh-unto miraculous, invaluable experience at hand.

No mountains – Then, after attending to meditation on mountains, one finds "mu" (no, nothing) and "sunyata" (empty, void, dependent arising, non-inherency), wherein there are no mountains, no "inherent," self-contained mountains, after all.

Mountains – As a result, the perspective then shifts – something like Monet's Haystacks – whereby the mountains are once again mountains, fostering and truly appreciating the value of a new way of seeing mountains wholistically, their 'what is' nature. There is a oneness of everything, including the subject/object, observer/observed phenomena. There is only the great equalizer: "nothing, "impermanence." Yes, things exist, but not inherently so; only correlatively, interdependently, as co-originating.

Part V

How? – Philosophical Journey
into Zen Buddhism

11. Philosophical Journey, in Depth

Zen:

"Zen" (Ch'an): The term means "meditation." And, in turn, 'Zen Buddhism' can be understood as 'meditation Buddhism.' The practice of Zen, more or less synonymous with Buddhism, in everyday life can be realized in sitting, walking, etc. For me, who did not start practicing zazen (sitting meditation) until two years ago, excused myself with what I had declared: Not sitting Zen or walking Zen, but "reading Zen," as I like to call it. I have been practicing "reading Zen" for innumerable years, to the point where, according to the Zen master's quip, I "stink of Zen."

A Zen perception of words:

Again, "words." Words played with by zennists, particularly exemplified in "koans," intellectual puzzles intended to dismantle the reflexive tendencies of ratiocination on the part of the recipient, the student. Language, as understood within a Zen context, serves us in a conventional, rhetorical sense for navigating through the practical activities and figures of speech in general commerce with people. However, there is more involved in grasping the ultimate truths of reality, more to life than meets the eye, something besides merely conventional truths. A famous Zen saying comes to mind: "Do not mistake the finger for the moon." For, words – "the finger" – "should not be mistaken for the "moon" – ultimate nature. To Zen Buddhism's credit, describing the world in myriad ways best encapsulates, for me, the hermeneutical reality of Wallace Stevens's phenomenological poem, in more detail:

Thirteen Ways of Looking at a Blackbird, Wallace Stevens (from the Poetry Foundation):

I

Among twenty snowy mountains,

The only moving thing

Was the eye of the blackbird.

II

I was of three minds,

Like a tree

In which there are three blackbirds.

III

The blackbird whirled in the autumn winds.

It was a small part of the pantomime.

IV

A man and a woman

Are one.

A man and a woman and a blackbird

Are one.

V

I do not know which to prefer,

The beauty of inflections

Or the beauty of innuendoes,

The blackbird whistling

Or just after.

VI

Icicles filled the long window

With barbaric glass.

The shadow of the blackbird

Crossed it, to and fro.

The mood

Traced in the shadow

An indecipherable cause.

VII

O thin men of Haddam,

Why do you imagine golden birds?

Do you not see how the blackbird

Walks around the feet

Of the women about you?

VIII

I know noble accents

And lucid, inescapable rhythms;

But I know, too,

That the blackbird is involved

In what I know.

IX

When the blackbird flew out of sight,

It marked the edge

Of one of many circles.

X

At the sight of blackbirds

Flying in a green light,

Even the bawds of euphony

Would cry out sharply.

XI

He rode over Connecticut

In a glass coach.

Once, a fear pierced him,

In that he mistook

The shadow of his equipage

For blackbirds.

XII

The river is moving.

The blackbird must be flying.

XIII

It was evening all afternoon.

It was snowing

And it was going to snow.

The blackbird sat

In the cedar-limbs.

    For decades now, I have been working towards a Zen way of seeing, a phenomenological way of description, and I return to singer, Donovan, in more detail:

"There is a Mountain" ~ sung by 1960s folk musician, Donovan:

The lock upon my garden gate's a snail, that's what it is
The lock upon my garden gate's a snail, that's what it is
First there is a mountain, then there is no mountain, then there is

First there is a mountain, then there is no mountain,
then there is
The caterpillar sheds his skin to find a butterfly within
Caterpillar sheds his skin to find a butterfly within
First there is a mountain, then there is no mountain,
then there is
First there is a mountain, then there is no mountain
Oh Juanita, oh Juanita, oh Juanita, I call your name
Oh, the snow will be a blinding sight to see as it lies
on yonder hillside
The lock upon my garden gate's a snail, that's what it
is
The lock upon my garden gate's a snail, that's what it
is
Caterpillar sheds his skin to find a butterfly within
Caterpillar sheds his skin to find a butterfly within
First there is a mountain, then there is no mountain,
then there is
First there is a mountain, then there is no mountain,
then there is
First there is a mountain, then there is no mountain,
then there is

First there is a mountain, then there is no mountain, then there is.

I take these lyrics to allude to the stages of awareness, or the: first, before we study the dharma (teachings) of Zen (meditation), we see the world as phenomenal, as mountains appear, and we take it for granted, we think we know. Then, upon Zen meditation, we see the emptiness (mu, nothing, the dependent arising) of the phenomenal world, the mountains receding into non-inherent existence. And, finally, after Zen meditation, we once again see mountains as mountains, as they truly are – a pure, direct experience of the phenomenal (appearances) and noumenal (ultimate) realms, seeing the underlying ultimate reality of the world, seeing the essence of mountains as if for the first time. As I like to say, "sometimes you've got to go up to get down."

Now, from a Westernized deconstructive, or postmodern, angle, Zen Buddhism may be accused of what is known as "essentialism," the notion that we can, indeed, experience and interpret life in a pure, unmediated, direct manner, in spite of any linguistic and hermeneutical, interpretive obstacles. While such an accusation of "essentialism" has left me in turmoil for innumerable years, I have finally landed on the side of confidence and stability in the human capacity to have pure, direct, unmediated experiences, in accordance with Zen Buddhist claims. I have come to my senses, finally. I have drunk from the Kool-Aid, perhaps, but it has a ring of truth for me, more than ever before. Shades of this confidence can be reflected in some pithy remarks I made ten years ago: "Nature is my sanctuary, and poetry my Bible; the last bastions of metaphysical comfort I refuse to deconstruct."

I'm gradually feeling more and more emotionally liberated, especially recently, as I have now declared to my loved ones that, "I guess I'm a Zen Buddhist after all." This is a huge, kind of scary, commitment for me to make, much less announce. But with zazen (sitting meditation) now becoming prominent in my life for the past two years, it is a Johnny-come-lately development on my part. I find Zen Buddhism to be endlessly fascinating from a philosophical and psychological standpoint, even though it is neither a philosophy nor a psychology. Nonetheless, it has the most penetrating set of philosophical and psychological analyses regarding life that I have ever come across. So, it works for me. Neither is Buddhism a religion, although it has some spiritually rewarding aspects to it. And, again, it works for me. All because of my desire to step off the merry-go-round, hermeneutically speaking, and to embrace transiency, non-solidity, impermanence, ambiguity.

I feel grounded in a non-grounding sort of way. Maybe not stepping off completely, but positioning myself to appreciate the myriad ways of perceiving within the merry-go-round, looking at life in a more Nietzschean manner of what is known as 'perspectivism.' Perspectivism is looking at life from multiple perspectives, seeing through a prism, not from a singular, absolutist standpoint. I have concerted my life's energies toward the endeavor of peering through a psycho-spiritu-philosophical prism, after the manner of phenomenology and Zen, and appreciating the array of colors life presents.

Part VI (Section 1)

How? – Psychological Journey
into Zen Buddhism

12. Delving into the Psychotherapeutic Aspects of Zen Meditation for Me

Zen Buddhism proposes a unitive experience of existence, of reality. It's not something we must conjure up, force, or make happen; rather, that nondualistic unity always already 'is,' we have but to become 'aware' of this unitive reality, 'realizing' the Buddha nature (enlightened one) within. As I understand it, 'actualizing' our Buddha nature within comes down to a 'wake up!' call. There is nothing to strive for or attain; only mindfulness, being aware of being here now.

"Miracle, Coincidence, or Synchronicity? You make the call!"

It occurred to me one very late night, circa 1990's, while cerebrating about "la pictura grande," the big picture, the whole enchilada – with my brother. We had just eaten an exquisite meal of Spanish tapas. Upon leaving the restaurant, we continued cerebrating and celebrating while under a streetlamp; when, suddenly, the light went pitch black for a prescient moment, just as someone (most likely me, given my super dark propensities) uttered the word "death." That is my apocryphal version, anyway. This story best exemplifies, to my mind, the signs and symbols that we impute on life's events; the manner in which we interpret the uncanny, inexplicable moments or events happening to us, for us; especially, when what's happening to us enters the ethical domain of our existential crises.

"Miracle, coincidence, or synchronicity? You make the call!" This phrase of mine has served me well, as it underscores the serendipitous nature of interpretation(s), and perhaps it has been entertaining to some other loved ones. This miracle-coincidence-synchronicity equation requires from us a "call," "you make the call!" Again, "words." Word-symbols matter! It has been one of my steadfast (or stubborn?) set of metaphors for life; three, among multiple, hermeneutical ways or vantage points – like the imagery behind poet Wallace Stevens' "13 Ways to Look at a Blackbird" – from which to view and interpret the events, words, and actions at hand. I shan't delve into great detail as to the meaning and application of each of these three word-symbols' in my larger equation.

Suffice it to say that "miracle" connotes viewing various life events as happenings that are nothing short of the uncanny, miraculous, and intervening manner of events; miracles necessarily violate the laws of nature. Sometimes things around us just appear out of nowhere, in a seemingly interceding fashion, out of the blue, taking us by surprise, stymied by life's inexplicable events.

"Coincidence" captures another way of seeing, viewing life's seemingly coincidental moments as just sheer luck, dumb luck, sometimes "buzzard luck" (thanks, Chris), totally unrelated events, after all. Charging life's events with coincidence lends a look at life as borne out of serendipity, chance happenings.

"Synchronicity" alludes to the Jungian school of psychology, whereby coinciding events happen to us within our collective unconscious as being meant to be, a synchronic simpatico between me and the universe, whereby circumstances "appear meaningfully related yet lack a causal connection." (Wikipedia).

"You make the call!" This refers to the exclamatory, hyperbolic reaction and manner in which we react to life's events, having myriad ways to interpret the data at hand at our disposal, more or less; reactions on our part that sometimes seem destined, maybe even predestined – "condemned to be free" (Sartre) – and requiring of us, the observer, a reaction, often times of ethical import, reaction(s) that desperately reach out for help as to how to interpret what is happening, and faced with a smorgasbord of interpretive lenses through which to ascertain what to do, how to react.

My intention behind the coinage of such a phrase was meant to express merely that we all encounter myriad ways of seeing reality, varying ways to interpret and appropriate to our worldview's liking. It is we – you and me and everybody else – who make the call, who impute and project meaning onto life's happenings. And, in turn, the happenings project on us. This way of looking at life demands our getting a hermeneutical, interpretive, lay of the land, and an interpretative handle to latch on to, so that we can best navigate the understanding(s) of happenings, of existence.

Hermeneutics – the theories of interpretation – is a vibrant field of study in Western philosophy, one which I have devoted much attention and interest. Beginning with Friedrich Schleiermacher in the 18th century – a philosopher and theologian, par excellence – a philosophical focus was cultivated such as to better understand the nature and processes of interpretation, especially in Christian theology and interpretation, which spawned the need for hermeneutics to begin with. Hermeneutics was needed to carry out biblical exegesis and interpretation. Hermeneutics attempts to examine the undergirding assumptions or presuppositions that the reader of the text – Christian and otherwise – carries into the process of interpretation. And everything is a "text" (Derrida) to be interpreted – words, people, events.

The "hermeneutical circle" or spiral is such that we can only understand the whole by understanding its parts, and equally so, we can only understand the parts by understanding its whole. The observer, or subject, (us), must ascertain the object of interpretation by way of both principles. There is no getting around the fact that inductive and deductive logics are required in order to understand something. For example, take picking up and reading a book. We approach the text with a set of presuppositions, some unbeknownst to us, that shape and color our understanding of the text. Some are in fact guiding questions that help us to better ascertain what the author and text are getting at. We bring all of this into the hermeneutical picture, three components: 1) authorial intent, 2) text, and 3) audience response. Put another way, as hermeneutics is not only involved with interpreting a book, but with interpreting all of life's events, we find another exemplification in the field of aesthetics (art), that hermeneutical understanding entails 1) the artist intent, 2) the work of art, and 3) its entry into the public domain of art appreciators (who either credit or discredit the art work, age after age). It ebbs and flows with the Zeitgeist of all generations.

Hermeneutics comes from the Greek god Hermes – message sender. He's the one who has wings on his heels. So, hermeneutics is all about the nature and process of interpretation; understanding, that is, piercing the veil into the nature of existence. All we can do, of course, is to follow the dictates of epistemological principles of induction, deduction, intuition, while synthetic-a priori-ing are way to a place of understanding, to see the overall picture, la pictura grande.

Hermeneutics. Why, for me? The recurring theme of "words," if I had to hazard a guess. I have had a burning desire to plumb the depths of hermeneutical theories of interpretation much of my life. I'm guessing that this ever so serious desire was borne out of the tumultuous years of my childhood, ages 10 to 12; borne out of the need to understand and come to grips with my father's premature death.

A lot of my life has been spent dutifully practicing the study of words written by philosophers, religionists, and psychologists. The driving force behind my intense interests in these linguistical areas was borne out of a deep-seated mistrust of people, and people's "words." I so mistrusted life, in general. In a word, what I was up to was hermeneutics – theories of interpretation, interpretations of "speech acts," framing and reframing the hermeneutical lenses, my perceptions of life. It was in this field of study that my imagination thrived the most. Especially, the twin-traditions within the history of Western philosophy: "hermeneutics of suspicion" and "hermeneutics of trust." Suspicion after the manner of Nietzsche, Marx, and Freud; and trust, or faith, after the manner of suspending judgement while under the temporary spell of "words;" movies being a good example. An example of the place of faith or trust can be found in watching films. When walking into a movie theatre, ready to face a film that you perhaps have heard about but never seen, you just allow the film to convey whatever it wants. It's just like opening a book you've never read before. Same hermeneutical rules apply: We must utilize a "hermeneutics of trust," or faith, as well as a "hermeneutics of suspicion." Faith that there is something worth sticking around for, a sympathetic gesture on our part to suspend criticism, or outright disbelief, in order to allow the life event to be approached credibly, nonjudgmentally. Only then does it behoove one to apply a healthy amount of suspicion and criticism, to stay objective.

Now, life's propositions, and/or existential givens, thrust themselves upon us, uninvited, and shape our decisions and worldviews, philosophically, psychologically, and ethically. There is an existential "thrownness" in two directions, as I see it. Life's propositions appear to be both a referent to our being thrown into the world without being asked to be born, as well as the world being thrown into us, like some kind of Sartrean "thrownness" in forward and reverse.

It is as if we are caught in a dream, mostly a bad dream, nightmarish, and powerless to control the outcome; it does what it does and we Homo sapiens are just along for the ride, so I thought.

No small wonder that, years spanning a lifetime, I have immersed myself in the films of Swedish director Ingmar Bergman, films which portray the angst-filled lives we lead. Today, I still treasure Bergman's films as both penetrating and cathartic. I wrote a Harvard Extension term paper on Bergman, entitled "From Crisis to Catharsis: The Poetic Nihilist 'Persona' of Ingmar Bergman."

Three Serviceable Psychological Equations:

The *Julie equation*: Pain + nonacceptance = suffering. Pain + acceptance = healing, letting go.

Julie guided me through two major issues: First, to love myself, that it was okay to love myself; and, second, she helped me to cultivate a sense of gratitude. It took the better part of five years of therapy, but gradually I came around. This was huge! I never had loved myself, and thought it hokey, the whole idea of loving yourself. Seemed so narcissistic and prideful; so, I wrote it off for a large part of my life, even though, ironically, I was the most narcissistic, self-centered person I knew.

Julie's DBT (Dialectical Behavioral Therapy) skills, partially sprung from CBT (Cognitive Behavioral Therapy), were for me, highly successful. I do love myself now . . . though, not falling in love with, of course. And I am grateful to be alive now . . . though, sans the goddesses and gods to thank. DBT is different from traditional psychodynamic therapy; no microscopic exhuming of the past, which I hear can take a lifetime, or lifetimes of therapy. Instead, Julie met me where my psychological needs were at, in the present, in the now, and matched it with DBT principles. She skillfully guided me to places of safety, junctures that there was nothing to be afraid of. It was at such junctures – amidst spaces of emotional upheaval – that I felt comfortable enough to bare all; nothing about my dark, "shadow self" was out of bounds.

I remember one DBT diagram Julie explained to me regarding the three spheres or domains of our mind: 1) Emotional mind, 2) rational mind, and 3) wise mind. The wise mind is the heart center, the core capacity that only needs to be awakened, much like the Buddha nature within. The wise mind processes and cultivates the grand narrative behind the multiple narratives that vie for first in place. The wise mind processes the life experiences at hand, and gives us a centeredness, with equanimity, an even-tempered mind and composure. In my case, I wished to awaken the Buddha nature within me; awaken the wise mind to guide me.

In connection with that diagram, I wrote up my own schemata of all the aspects of life that I consider to be Reservoirs of Solace for My Heart and Wise Mind, and shared it with Julie. I can best describe it as a kind of logotherapeutic (recalling Victor Frankl's "logotherapy") set of "word" devices that I devised to fortify and center me. Thank you my good friend, Susan, for giving me one of the thought-provoking reservoirs – "from something to something." My reservoirs go like this, in no particular order:

Reservoirs Of Solace For My Heart

and Wise Mind

***

"Miracle, coincidence, or synchronicity?

You make the call!"

Serenity prayer

Tathata = suchness, thusness

"We all get there"

Friends and loved ones

Zen Buddhism

Music & Art

Poetry

Nature

"For As Long as I Am Alive!"

"That's What Doctors and Hospitals Are For"

"The Whole World's A Hospital –

You Can Either Be a Patient

or You Can Be a Nurse"

"From Nothing to Nothing"

"From Something to Something"

I shall not go into any of the details about these reservoirs, but suffice it to say, these cathartic reservoirs, these hermeneutic lenses, do assist me – like mental tapes I would play throughout my life.

The *Andy equation*: Forbid foreboding and forbid the forbidding of feeling carefree.

Recently, I opened my therapy session with Andy by introducing him to a recent discovery I had made regarding coping mechanisms; I found this pretty helpful, "forbid foreboding." I actually found just the right tool by realizing that everybody has a forbidden zone. You know, some families don't talk politics or religion. So why can't I have such a "zone," having lived my life like something out of the Twilight Zone. And at the '11th hour' of our session, Andy submitted that it sounded to him like there were other things that I was forbidding. I went home with that thought, and toyed over it for a few days (like it was some kind of a koan), managing to create an equation, "forbid the forbidding of feeling carefree." I have Andy to thank for turning me around completely. So, I have amassed two "forbids": forbid foreboding, and forbid the forbidding of feeling carefree. And because I like the results, I shall widen the net to what other "forbids" I should possibly maintain for my psychological wellbeing.

In the next session, I shared with Andy what I had discovered. In turn, he guided me through a process in which it was okay for me to feel carefree, regardless of life's ceaseless, unrelenting maladies, calamities, impending doom, and ultimate demise that visits us all, always, never not. This, coupled with Andy's therapeutic approach, which is steeped in Eastern wisdom and otherwise, while I, too, am steeped in Buddhist psychology.

Andy introduced me to the psychologist Erik Erikson writings concerning "Competencies vs. Inadequacies" over a normal life span; a table Erikson devised, entitled *Life Stages and Development Imperatives*. Evidently, my childhood ages 10 to 12 missed out on the competencies that are normally expected to be developed between ages 8 to 12. In my childhood turmoil, I missed out on so many important competencies; for I was always thinking and feeling I would never amount to anything, never be successful, always inadequate. As a result of this table, my therapist and I are working on developing the competencies or skills I missed out on. I can only say, lucky me. I found a great shrink, right up there with Julie. And right down here in my little ol' town! "Forbid foreboding." And "forbid the forbidding of feeling carefree."

The **Allan equation**: Pain + attachment = suffering.

Allan guided me through the Buddha's "Four Noble Truths" and the Noble Eight-Fold Path in an 8-week workshop that a good friend, Ana, pointed me to. In Allan's Buddhistic equation, circa 2022, directed at my question regarding the 'why' of suffering, my tortured mind was finally set at rest. Attachment was the culpable culprit! After decades of carrying around this weighty problematic of 'why evil and suffering?' which became my resentful resolve for a lifetime of existential revolt over what is known in philosophy and religion circles as the classic 'problem of evil and suffering.' I had had a longstanding resentment towards god/dess, and even towards life itself. God/dess, or life, just didn't seem to be fair when it came to its existential demands of suffering, and ultimately death, the great equalizer.

How could and why would an all-powerful (omnipotent), all-knowing (omniscient), and all-loving (omnibenevolent) god/dess create, or at least permit, life's unbearable tragedies as the price we humans pay for having a free will agency, the ability to choose, to choose obedience or rebellion against a lord/dess, thus, our deciding our future (heaven or hell)?

In his workshop, Allan presented the challenging prospect of a Buddhistic remedy: Pain plus attachment = suffering. According to the Buddha's First Noble Truth, life is suffering. Pain just is. Such is life. Suffering (Pali: dukkha), however, has an origin in human ignorance and unquenchable desire, clinging onto earthy possessions of all forms, allowing attachments to become deep-seated, fighting tooth and nail against a battle that is uneven, death being an 'uneven battle,' from the alpha and omega of life's trajectory. Ignorance and desire are the origin and promulgating variables entailed therein, that causes suffering. If we were not so attached to Maya – the ephemeral ever-elusive, illusion of "permanence" and "solidity" – we would experience a much different life in the making.

For me, Buddhism makes the most sense, intuitively; there's a proverbial ring of truth in my ears, philosophically and psychologically. In Pali, the term Buddhism uses is "anicca," impermanence. All of life is forever changing, always in transition, always adapting and morphing. Our desperate clinging onto life's pleasures and treasures as being somehow "permanent," is, as it turns out, a misguided perception we have of reality. There is no permanent permanence (pardon the redundancy), only the transitory. Or, as one of my friends, Jared, told me repeatedly, echoing the Bible's *Book of Ecclesiastes*, "life is a vapor," "all is futility." If we can just accept life on its terms of transitoriness, we would be much more at peace with life as we know it, I think. For me, it works. It does it's not-so-supernatural – but nevertheless uncanny – magical, restorative work on me; such that my whole psychological façade was melted away. I had finally realized that my whole life was preparing me for this newfound existential resolve; a resolve that I had longed for my entire life. I still embrace a Nietzschean form of perspectivism, i.e., the holding together multiple perspectives at once. But I now have at my disposal a unique set of tools, coping mechanisms, really – after 25 years of my pouring over Zen Buddhist literature – that have provided a real source of relief; resolve and relief, philosophically, spiritually, and psychologically, even though Zen Buddhism is none of these things.

Oh, the lacunas, the psychological blinders, we all put on to protect ourselves from the weight of the world, recalling Beat poet Allen Ginsberg, who wrote "the weight of the world is love." Camus wrote something not too dissimilar in sentiment, "The struggle itself toward the heights is enough to fill a man's heart. One must imagine Sisyphus happy," the last two lines of his "Myth of Sisyphus." For, "this is it," as Alan Watts reminds us in his book "This Is It," and that has to be "enough." I bow to the Nietzschean dictum, "amor fati," love your fate. As well, C. D. Keyes's lover of fate and "poetic nihilist," as opposed to the "cynic nihilist," has shaped my viewpoint. To paraphrase Keyes, sure, we are all sinking, inevitably, in the existential lifeboat. But whereas the cynic nihilist proceeds, out of frustration and existential revolt, to punch more holes in the sinking lifeboat, the poetic nihilist has a reckoning and decides to write a song or a sonnet, instead. This Buddhistic tathata – or suchness and thusness of life, life on its terms – may not look like enough, but it has to be. For me.

Watts's book, *This is It,* bears repeating. It's a different kind of IT, but a softer, gentler IT, to replace the surreal, sterilized, isolating, alienating IT, the face of *Death*." It's a supple, bending and bowing *Death*, instead of an inflexible, indifferent, assaultive, out to get you IT. And, so, I come now to the hermeneutical table with a Buddhistic non-discriminating mind, a "non-difference" (but not indifference) and interdependency of what just is, without discrimination of good or bad, happy or sad. As Derrida and phenomenologist John D. Caputo put it – "es gibt," "it happens," "it gives," without the emotional disassociation that the old indifferent IT had had over me. Buddhism, to my understanding, embraces the universe as it just IS, tathata, the suchness and thusness of life, without the need to pray to a god/dess for forgiveness or for divine intervention.

The Buddha nature within all of us sentient beings (Buddha means "enlightened one") allows the potentiality for our awakening and getting through all that life entails, for good or ill. It's the Buddhistic dukkha (life is suffering) that we all face. Dukkha is the "weight" we encounter as a result of "love," for we love and care for ourselves and others, and that concern is necessarily weighty in many respects; the existential challenges to each and every one of us countlessly, and, yet, "one must imagine Sisyphus happy;" that is, if we follow the path of the "poetic nihilist," without the cynicism of the "cynic nihilist," instead, loving our fate and living without regrets. It is having Tillich's "courage to be," in spite of the existential threats and ultimate demise of all sentient beings. As existential psychoanalyst Irvin Yalom describes, there are "existential givens" that we all have to face and hopefully resolve, in order to live out a meaningful and satisfactory life – *Death* being just such an existential given. *Death* is a non-personified, nonanthropomorphic IT; life just IS, "it happens." *Death* just IS, es gibt. It happens, one might even say "shit happens," depending on one's point of view. IT IS. Where we get into trouble is when we attempt to anthropomorphize IT with a bunch of images and names of god/desses that are actually projections of our human imagination (according to philosopher Ludwig Feuerbach), projecting on to the god/dess our "human, all too human" (Nietzsche) characteristics, and create a laundry list of a 'do's and don't's' as to what pleases the god/dess; a deeply embedded human urge to appease the god/esses. On the other hand, perhaps it's okay that human languages just do the best they can to name the universe, designating names for the universes, of which we are part, albeit, infinitesimally small and brief compared to galactic time.

Part VI (Section 2)

How? – Psychological Journey
into Zen Buddhism

13. Psychological Journey, Exegesis in Depth

Of primary interest to me for innumerable years has been the studying of 'Buddhist psychology,' specifically examining where Eastern meets Western views of the human psyche meet. While Western psychology has made quantum leaps in unpacking the psyche through psychoanalysis, the Eastern wisdom of Buddhism goes the deepest, I think, in ascertaining the root cause – and the remedy – for human suffering within the psycho-spiritu-philosophical domains. That said, Buddhism is not a psychology, per se. As closest to a Western mindset's way of thinking, Zen Buddhism can be considered a form of psychology, offering tools for coping, more than anything else. For, Zen Buddhism presents analyses of the 'human condition,' starting with diagnoses, and then therapies, after the manner of doing psychology – analyzing in detail the contributing psychological factors that comprise the human psyche.

In the remainder of this work, I shall underscore some of the salient points of Buddhist psychology, and how they have impacted me, all for the better. I shall include italicized, boldface captions for the "Summation" and "Personal Takeaways" for each author. This not being a technical, academic treatise, I have dropped the use of exacting quotation marks. Instead, I present to the reader my adaptation, paraphrasing what each author is saying; including the personal takeaways of what I have come to believe. I string together adapted, partial quotes from each author, along with pagination in parentheses, and include my personal takeaways of what I believe the author is getting at. There is a measure of my "reading into" the authors, but I like to believe that I do a fair bit of justice to them. I take on this hermeneutical exercise with the hopes of further deepening my own heartfelt relationship with Zen Buddhism, and, of course, to pique the interests of the reader.

Here are the most defining works that I have studied on the subject matter of 'Buddhist psychology,' in the order that I first read them:

1) *The Iron Cow of Zen ~ Albert Low*

2) *Psychotherapy East and West ~ Alan Watts*

3) *Zen Therapy: Transcending the Sorrows of the Human Mind ~ David Brazier*

4) *Thoughts Without a Thinker: Psychotherapy from a Buddhist Perspective ~ Mark Epstein*

5) *The Couch and the Tree: Dialogues in Psychoanalysis and Buddhism ~ Anthony Molino, ed.*

6) *Awakening the Heart: East/West Approaches to Psychotherapy and the Healing Relationship* ~ *John Welwood, ed.*

7) *How To See Yourself as You Really Are* ~ *The 14th Dalai Lama (Tenzin Gyatso)*

Now on to my psychological exegesis of the Zen Buddhist psychology books that have helped me immensely.

Book 1) *The Iron Cow of Zen* ~ Albert Low

Summation:

In Albert Low's work, he states that Zen is not a philosophy, religion, or psychology; instead, it is a practice (12); a practice of awakening the Buddha nature within. Buddha means "awakened one" (12).

95

And everyone has the capacity of Buddha nature; we must only awaken it.

Now, Low begins by describing the human condition as entailing three companions: Sickness, old age, and death (23). And we encounter three companions of uncertainty, impermanence, and lack (26). In Buddhism, such a state of affairs is called dukkha, suffering (121). The 'Way' entails pain, uncertainties, and ambiguities that are non-negotiable (161). And the iron cow of mu (nothing) dispels our dreams of any eureka, any escape (196).

Low suggests that life is a "vertigo of transience" (10), a state of ambiguity that actually leads to a state of non-ambiguity (15). It involves the Gordian knot – insoluble problems – whereby nothing is unambiguous (74). We appear to be in search of an unambiguous Other (72), but the Gordian knot is an intractable problem (189), whereby we live our lives both as "me-as-center and me-as-periphery" (97, 100). Our reality is to live as center and periphery (66-68) in a simultaneity of moments. For Low, ego is the unholy alliance of center, of uniqueness (158).

In quantum physics, the Niels Bohr principle of complementarity provides the epistemological basis for indeterminacy (57). And it is useless to seek out and imagine oneself as finding any absolute truth, absolute rest (150). Instead, we must suffer the ambiguities (149), for it is in vain to try to find an absolute center or ultimate value (149). We human beings are ordinary (32), nothing special.

Low points out something that Heidegger wrote, "We are a conversation" (127). (Heidegger, in another place, describes language as the "house of Being," and that language thinks us more than we think language.) Within Buddhism's framework, we come to realize the truth of our arising, mutual dependency (73); an interdependency, as opposed to some autonomous, free-floating ego.

Zen Buddhism is not a matter of emptying mind but seeing into mind (51), in order to experience enlightenment (95). Such enlightenment can be summed up in a most puzzling, yet brilliant, Zen saying by Lin-chi, "If you meet the Buddha, kill him" (117). That is to say, if you think you have found a spiritual guru outside of yourself to save you, you are in error. Instead, we must embrace self-reliance, trusting that each of us has the Buddha nature necessary to overcome obstacles, if only we awaken it. The Buddha nature is not a belief in, or worship of, some kind of savior god/dess.

Personal Takeaways:

Low's Iron Cow of Zen speaks volumes for me, it being one of my earliest books I had read concerning Zen Buddhism. In his use of a 'center-periphery' metaphor – representing the simultaneous twin-domains of me-as-center, me-as-periphery – I continue to find it a compelling model for ascertaining the common exchange and dynamic of "words" that pass between people. Hermeneutics comes in to play, both self-centered and other-centered, the twin-foci of the human interpretation and experience.

Also of great importance to me is Low's underscoring of the ambiguous/non-ambiguous vertigo of transience that is found in our acts of interpretation. For, "now we see through a glass darkly," always confined to the impermanence of human interpretation owing to the finite and feebleness of human language and understanding.

Finally, I have forever been intrigued by Lin-chi's startling assertion, "If you meet the Buddha, kill him!" What on earth could that mean? As psychologist Sheldon Kopp explains in his work, using this quote as his title, if you meet/follow a guru to somehow "save" you, you are in error. As Low underscores, do not blithely follow an outside Buddha for liberation; instead, you must awaken the Buddha nature (enlightened one) within; Zen Buddhism is all about self-reliance. As my good friend, Bill, says (quoting from somewhere), "no-one likes a cold stove."

Book 2) *Psychotherapy East and West* ~ Alan Watts

Summation:

Watt's "Psychotherapy East and West" was one of my first books to read about Zen Buddhism; the first being his "The Way of Zen," an outstanding work providing a readable, lucid introduction to Zen.

Watts delineates two alternate universes: The West's way of seeing life via a dualistic psychology; and the East's way of seeing life via liberation, the way of liberation (3-4). It is liberation from egocentrism (61) most importantly; liberation from social institutions, but not from the physical world (48); liberation from a dualistic view of psyche (98). But, that said, liberation is not quitting society (76); rather, it is active engagement in the world of suffering, fostering and providing solace and alleviation from the fact that, in accordance with the Buddha's First Noble Truth, that life is suffering. Liberation is, in fact, release from the dualistic split we have falsely created all around us, Watts suggests (173). A quick, but noteworthy, aside:

For Watts, Western Existentialism comes closest to Eastern liberation (111).

Western tendencies toward dualistic thinking – although, great strides have been made in the Western way of seeing – end up falling into a false sense of 'I,' as if the subjective 'I' were separate and outside of external reality. But for Watts, such a skin-encapsulated ego is a false view (11), for there is no skin-encapsulated 'I' (145). Instead, it is a "mythical 'I,' a supposed 'I' that, ironically, is actually controlled by others (80-81). The apparent independence of ourselves is a matter of social convention for Watts (67), a relative truth, but not ultimately so. The notion of a thinker behind the thoughts is, for Watts, an illusion (133). We must cease identifying with ego (160).

For Zen Buddhism, the task is not to further isolate this so-called autonomous 'I' or ego, but to foster a sense of interdependency and continuity. It is a unitive vision of reality; a vision that is non-fragmentary; a reality of interdependency. Watts indicates in another book, that the sun needs us (the human eye) as much as we need the sun.

When it comes to understanding and diagnosing what ails the world, Zen Buddhism is starkly contrasted from the West, the West with its Judeo-Christian proclivities; for Zen Buddhism, the diagnosis is that human beings are not sinful, but sick. Sick rather than sinful, Watts suggests (163). Furthermore, it's time we stop taking life seriously and continue to play (184). The origin of suffering is not sinfulness, but human ignorance and desire. Desire is the cause of anguish, Watts states (135).

To disabuse the reader of any wrongful assumptions about the human condition and the human task at hand, the Zen Buddhist's prime directive is to alleviate suffering wherever it is found. Also, the task is not to destroy maya but see through it (9). Within the perspective of Zen Buddhism, the task is attaining Nirvana, the release from samsara (the cycle of birth, death, rebirth), Watts points out (16). These tasks are all to be accomplished with wu-hsin, no mind (38-39). This, in turn, 'let's his mind think whatever it likes' (139).

As to other beliefs of the zennist, such as karma and reincarnation, Watts suggests that reincarnation and miracles are to be understood symbolically, not literally (59).

Personal Takeaways:

While liberating myself, in degrees, from a strictly Westernized tradition of dualistic thinking, I am nevertheless ensconced with a habituated thinking that is resultant of Platonic and Cartesian dualisms; seeing and interpreting the universe in dichotomous ways, a subject-object view of reality, and a divided, dualistic psyche. This distortion creates a philosophical and psychological chasm between the subject (us the observer) and the object (external reality). This dualistic distortion of existence ipso facto distances us from the world and creates a false sense of fragmentation within the human experience of the world all around us. Lost is the continuity and interdependence of life. It is like a friend/foe kind of split that pits the personal (subject) against the impersonal foreign external (object), all in an effort to dominate and command external reality, thereby seemingly bending external reality to our liking. But in the Eastern mindset, the world is not meant to be conquered or dominated. From the Eastern point of view, tathata – the suchness, thusness of life, as Watts translates it – reflects the truth at hand, that we must take all of life on terms that we may not always wish. We must be the twig that bends with the force of the water current; otherwise, we snap. Mindful of what the Western world's Voltaire posited, we must be good stewards upon this earth, cultivating our garden. Such a cultivating spirit and practice is indicative of the East, it comes naturally.

Are we sick or are we sinful? Speaking in generalities, the East's Buddhistic diagnosis renders ignorance and desire as the origin of suffering, and that wins the day for me. While I've ducked in and out – mostly out – of religious leanings throughout my life, having such ludicrous and unhelpful doctrines as 'original sin,' it is my immediate past – two years of zazen (sitting meditation) and 25 years of studying Zen Buddhist philosophy and psychology – that I wish to underscore. Unbeknownst to me, all these years I was practicing what I called "reading zen," somewhat satirically, instead of the customary 'sitting zen.' Evidently, I've been loosely practicing 'gufu-shogyo-zen,' a Zen tradition for novices to earnestly study Zen tenets and principles, a 'fool's zen,' it is called, but nevertheless Zen.

Unitive vision also rings true to me; that, rather than any mind/body dichotomies, or a skin-encapsulated 'I.' I am deeply impacted by the Eastern view of the human condition; that, what ails us (ignorance) and what remedy's us (meditation) fully addresses the human situatedness.

Book 3) *Zen Therapy: Transcending the Sorrows of the Human Mind* **~ David Brazier**

Summation:

For Brazier, dukkha (suffering) tells us we need to do something (13). But everything that happens is a doorway to liberation (14). One could view Zen as psychotherapy, freedom from conditioning (21, 59). That said, it is also the case that Buddhist liberation is different from psychological adjustment (30). Buddhist psychology is an analysis of conditioning (77). Japanese Morita therapy uses some Zen principles, but not to rid our problems; rather, how to live well despite our problems (108). And Japanese Naikan therapy, somewhat akin to Morita therapy, entails one-week retreat-like conditions (131) in order to assist the patient in awakening the Buddha nature within, to have the patient cultivate a garden, to establish self-reliance, without any outside, divine rescuer.

According to Brazier, prajna (wisdom) approximates the term diagnosis (215). And the key ingredient is to practice self-surrender unto harmony (229). As well, one must surrender to the greater power beyond self (255), placing trust in Self. This Self connotes something different than self; Self is synonymous with Buddha nature. It is a matter of owning up to our own competency, our Buddha nature within. Sense the universe is whole, we are part of something greater than self (33). The objective is to decondition ourselves by way of Zen (34). In this Buddhistic framework, there is no such thing as sin, only ignorance (185).

For Brazier, the natural person is ethical (44) and there is a body-mind unity (136), and taming of the mind (178). It is an emptying rather than filling (208) that takes place. Therein, we find that compassion means unconditional acceptance (195) of ourselves and others.

Brazier proposes two forms of Zen practice: Meditation on your own decomposing body (98), and making use of koans to help one shift out of self-centeredness (105).

Personal Takeaways:

I wholeheartedly agree with the correlation Brazier makes between psychoanalysis and Zen Buddhism, that Zen provides a kind of psychoanalytic diagnosis. Outside of this, there is no ultimate rescuer, as much as one might wish that there were.

Buddhist psychology submits that compassion is required, that compassion amounts to unconditional acceptance. This is true for me, at least part of the time. My therapy with Julie taught me that it was okay to have compassion for myself and others; she introduced me to a concept called 'radical acceptance.'

Book 4) *Thoughts Without a Thinker: Psychotherapy from a Buddhist Perspective* ~ **Mark Epstein**

Summation:

In this work, Epstein underscores the fact that life is suffering, it is dukkha, the suffering and dissatisfaction in life (46). The cause of dukkha is craving (59). The human condition is narcissistic (69), but neuroses that derive from narcissism can be transformed (79). Before the arrival of Western psychology, Buddhism perfected the uprooting of narcissism (4), along with the tendency to cling (62). The human psyche can be freed from narcissism (41). However, we experience an existential insecurity (55) that seems insurmountable. Buddhist psychology takes such identity confusion as the starting point (6). As a matter of fact, Epstein mentions that William James was impressed with the psychological sophistication of Buddhism (1).

Epstein remarks that the self is a fiction (87), the absence of self-sufficiency (100). It behooves us to attain a non-judgmental mindset, practicing bare awareness (113). The Buddhist practice of meditation can act as a remedy for what ails us. Meditation deconstructs the self (129), but is not world-denying (3). In fact, it can open us to experience the world around us directly (17). Awareness of our transitoriness leads to feeling more real (145). Buddhism is breath-based, not appetite-based (147).

Epstein highlights several other Buddhistic points worth mentioning in the context of Buddhist psychology. The Buddhist 'don't know' mind (56) involves a neither/nor logic (63) when examining existence. Through such practices, we can transform psychic disturbances into objects of meditation (127). As to the true nature of the erroneously "thinker" behind the "thoughts," we are just thoughts, just feelings (124); there is no thinker. For there is no 'inherently existent' I (125).

Personal Takeaways:

I take the Buddhist diagnosis of all sentient experiencing dukkha, suffering, to heart. For I have been plagued, emotionally and spiritually, for decades regarding the classic philosophical "problem of evil and suffering." That is to say, why suffering? Especially if there is a god/dess involved. And if a god/dess, how could it be possible – with so-called attributes of omniscience, omnipotence, and omnibenevolence – to reconcile it with the existence of pain and suffering? Wouldn't such a god/dess be able to create a better world than this? (Parenthetically, the so-called "free will" argument – that we were created with free will agency in order to freely worship god/dess or not – does not excuse god/dess from being responsible for natural disasters and the very existence of evil and suffering.)

The human condition is narcissistic, and uprooting narcissism is the task that lies before Buddhism. Some of the tools for uprooting such a self-serving mentality include realization that there is no 'inherently existent'

I. Further treatment would involve the application of the Zen principle of 'don't know' mind.

Book 5) *The Couch and the Tree: Dialogues in Psychoanalysis and Buddhism* ~ **Anthony Molino, editor; a collection of essayists**

<u>Joe Tom Sun:</u>

Summation:

Buddhists do not pray and there is no anthropomorphic intermediator (7).

Personal Takeaways:

Buddhism, while without the god/dessess, does present to us a knowing, and more importantly, experiencing, of a true essence – existence. All without anthropomorphizing – the erroneous projection of human characteristics, like jealousy or anger, onto the universe, or higher power.

W. Van Dusen:

Summation:

As Van Dusen remarks, the void is Zen's 'no mind' (56). Wu-wei (nonaction), coupled with a total uncertainty (57), is the appropriate response to appreciate "no mind." Thus, we realize the importance of a kind of action that is non-action, acting with skillful means, not mindless, reactionary actions. The void refers to the Buddhist notion of "mu," empty, nothing (but not the Western nihilistic notion of nothingness), whereby 'form is emptiness and emptiness is form.'

Personal Takeaways:

The void is "no mind." We can respond to the void by way of practicing wu-wei, non-action, just letting being be. This 'going with the flow' attitude is the most effective way to truly appreciate the nature of the universe. Psychologist Mihaly Csikszentmihalyi wrote a book entitled "Finding Flow: The Psychology of Engagement with Everyday Life," wherein he describes in detail how to find flow in the daily activities that regulate our lives.

Akihisa Kondo:

Summation:

As with the highly revered pronouncements of Dogen, it is the case that anxiety is the driving force to enlightenment (58). And enlightenment is the realizing of true self (60). Angst is the existential catalyst for the path of enlightenment, unveiling the bare essence of existence. This is enlightenment, revealing true Self or the Buddha nature within.

Personal Takeaways:

'Angst' is for me an existential anxiety, a foreboding, what I refer to as dead dread, as we face the existential facts of life, the "existential givens" (recalling here psychoanalyst Irvin Yalom). Anxiety – whether fortunately or not – becomes the catalyst for spiritual and emotional growth, as well as enlightenment.

Erich Fromm:

Summation:

Zen transcends ethics (67).

Personal Takeaways:

The ethical stage (my recalling Kierkegaard's three stages on life's way – aesthetic, ethical, and religious) is not sufficient to the task of self-transcending. Ethics is an intermediary stage on life's way, but not quite reaching the peak of religious, or spiritual, awareness, of enlightenment.

Harold Kelman:

Summation:

Western psychology tends to emphasize past and future, while the East emphasizes the absolute present (73). Now, if carried to its logical conclusion, the psychotherapeutic approach can roughly approximate an Eastern way of seeing (77). The chasm between Western and Eastern ways of perceiving existence is branched somewhat by the West's practice of psychotherapy, as it makes existential inquiries somewhat like the way of seeing in the Eastern Buddhism.

Personal Takeaways:

Be Here Now, a title of a popular book by Ram Dass, has become a motto for me, as I attempt to take to heart the forever 'present tense' of life. I believe that the past, as well as the future, is nothing other than a series of present moments. That's all we got, but isn't that enough, I ask myself? I like to think so, on my good days, at least.

I wholeheartedly believe in the partial wedding of psychotherapeutic techniques with Zen Buddhist tools, to break down the false constructs – our psychological armor – we erroneously erect in order to protect ourselves.

Takeo Doi:

Summation:

The Morita therapy of Japan (86) comes into the forefront of Japanese therapy. For Morita therapy, the mind ideally flows smoothly and continuously (92).

Personal Takeaways:

In Japan, Morita therapy has been very beneficial in grounding the patient – person, rather – in practical matters, like tilling a garden. The prime directive is to cultivate the garden at hand, at the place of retreat (sometimes having the person spend one week with the Morita therapist). This makes a lot of sense to me, highly practical and grounding.

Jack Engler:

Summation:

Experience all moments with equanimity (114). In Buddhism, one adopts an even-tempered response to each and every single moment encountered – good or bad, sun or rain.

Personal Takeaways:

In my life, I have often fought an uphill battle on how to not see rainy days any differently than sunny weather; more easily said than done. I feel that dealing with such days with equanimity is the best way for me to go. No good or bad days to pit against each other. Equanimity – a space in which to deal with life in an even-tempered manner.

Mark Epstein:

Summation:

Mindfulness leads to insight (121). And thought's insubstantiality (124), whereby the self is seen as not a fixed entity (125), must be appropriated into the Buddhist notion of anatta, no-soul, no-self (126).

Personal Takeaways:

Since thought is insubstantial, I must practice mindfulness in order to attain insight into anatta (no-soul, no-self). For, there is no such thing as an inherent existent 'I.'

V. Walter Odajnyk:

Summation:

Meditation starves and shrinks human drives (136). Meditation can and does alleviate neuroses (137).

Personal Takeaways:

Meditation is essential to minimizing the injurious impact and effects that our neuroses can have on us. Meditation can reduce the poisonous effects of neurotic behavior and perception.

Mark Finn:

Summation:

Buddhism is all about deliverance, not divine intervention (161). Additionally, it behooves us to reckon with a radical deconstruction of dualism (167), to go beyond dualistic, divisive thinking, and broaden our way of seeing the universe and ourselves.

Personal Takeaways:

For vast stretches of my life, I have felt a desperate need and urge for an "ultimate rescuer" (recalling existentialist psychoanalyst Irvin Yalom). My psychological needs have tended towards expectations of being saved, spared from a harsh, heartless world and, more importantly, saved from myself. This is a divisive way to look at the self and the universe, presuming a chasm between god/dess and humankind that must, then, be bridged by god/dess. This, in turn, created a vicious cycle, wherein I was always trying to pray my way through life's hardships. But it has been with the god/dessless Buddhist path that my heart feels most grounded, albeit a transitory groundedness.

Masao Abe:

Summation:

Anatman means no-self (183). And no-self is true Self (188).

Personal Takeaways:

No-self is true Self in the sense that one pierces through the veil of maya, realizing that at bedrock, there is no bedrock, just anicca, impermanence, transitoriness. This Buddhistic view towards the Self is not via the so-called autonomous, free-floating ego of the West. Rather, the Self is the self-transcending Self,

Paul C. Cooper:

Summation:

Emptiness is dependent arising (238).

Personal Takeaways:

In Buddhism, there is a guiding principle that everything, especially all sentient beings, is mu, nothing, emptiness. For, there can be no such thing as a inherent existent; rather, we are composed of aggregates, parts comprising the whole, whereby the "self" is maya, an illusion. We are comprised of dependent arisings (sometimes referred to as dependent co-arisings or co-origination), aggregates, parts, solely so. I think dependent arisings is the best rendering, for co- implies the distinction of two, sounding a little bit like dualism.

Stephen Kutz:

Summation:

Zen sees through illusion into reality itself (257).

Personal Takeaways:

Zen, or meditation, pierces the veil of appearances, perceiving into reality's true nature (I'm recalling the terms noumenal and phenomenal used by Kant, and later, Sartre).

Gereon Kopf:

Summation:

Selflessness transcends the subject-object dualistic thinking (286).

Personal Takeaways:

From a Buddhistic standpoint, it is through losing yourself (altruism) and performing compassionate acts of kindness that alleviating others' suffering becomes possible. In turn, such altruistic acts make it possible to transcend the maya of a subject-object dichotomy.

Joseph Bobrow:

Summation:

Suffering doesn't disappear; rather, our relation to suffering is subverted (316).

"Life is suffering" is the first of four truths in the Four Noble Truths presented by the historical Gautama Buddha, undermining the power of maya to delude us, subverting it in order to awaken our Buddha nature inside.

John R. Suler:

Summation:

Psychotherapy probes our paradoxes (327). The koan reveals our interdependency (332). Zen holds a paradoxical inseparability of relative and absolute truths (333).

Personal Takeaways:

As paradoxical as it seems, relative truths are conventions that we use in daily commerce, while universal truths are ultimate truths, truths of ultimate signification, peering into universal truths. Some people, like me, stumble over life's paradoxes, and especially antinomies, and it can require from me psychotherapeutic probing, which can be key to peering into paradoxical logic, without falling into a nihilistic quagmire.

Polly Young-Eisendrath:

Summation:

We must accept suffering and death (348). Suffering teaches us to take responsibility for each other's subjective lives (352).

Personal Takeaways:

Suffering and death are inevitabilities. But they can instruct us, if we accept the proposition of suffering, to accept the naked truth, and empathize with others who are suffering the same plight. We must love our neighbor as ourselves (Jesus), taking action to protect others, fellow sentient beings, from the harshness of suffering.

Book 6) *Awakening the Heart: East/West Approaches to Psychotherapy and the Healing Relationship* **~ John Welwood, editor; a collection of essayists**

<u>John Welwood:</u>

Summation:

Maitri means unconditional friendliness toward oneself (xiii).

Personal Takeaways:

Maitri refers to benevolence – towards others and self – as an unconditional, radical love and acceptance toward all sentient beings. I have always had a love/hate relationship with people, a misanthropy that I have now decidedly dropped, partially, at least. I now believe that, owing to the suffering that each person experiences – all people suffer, the situation demands of me a love and empathetic compassion to all sentient beings.

Jacob Needleman:

Summation:

An individual is a set of disconnected impulses, thoughts, sensations (12).

Personal Takeaways:

As I see it, all human beings are a bundle of conditionings, disconnected aggregates that make up our nature. It is much like, as the Dalai Lama explains (further down in my work), a table, which in itself does not exist; for it is comprised of parts, aggregates such as the legs, the table top, bolts, etc. The "table" is not an inherently existent. Rather, it is a composition of aggregates, parts. I am here mindful of the Western philosophical school of Nominalism, wherein universals are not considered to be real; rather, they are names only in our mind.

A.C. Robin Skynner:

Summation:

We are creatures of two worlds: Psychological traditions and the sacred traditions (31).

Personal Takeaways:

Human beings are living in the two domains of influence, twin-traditions that inform us – the psychological and the sacred, ritualistic traditions. Each has its advantages, providing insight into the core of what it means to be human.

Jack Kornfield, Ram Dass, Mokusen Miyuki:

Summation:

Psychology aims at getting people from unhappiness to happiness as the prime directive, while Buddhism comes to grip with the truth that all is suffering (35), there's nowhere to hide.

Personal Takeaways:

Although there is nowhere to hide, Buddhism does provide solace for and cessation from suffering by way of following the Four Noble Truths and the Noble Eight-Fold Path; truths and paths that liberate, enrich, and ground our lived experience.

John Welwood:

Summation:

Meditation is a way of inquiring into what the 'I' consists of (46). Letting go of 'I' fixation via meditation

(47) is liberating to the core. The East expands our lives beyond just psychological adjustment (51), and more into liberation. And it is advised that one must have a strong sense of self first, before transcending self (51). For, Eastern teachings assume that a person already has a healthy self-structure (52).

Personal Takeaways:

Here lies a critical point. The principles of Buddhism assume the recipient already has a core strength and fortitude of a 'self.' One must, it is assumed, first have a self to lose a self, must have a self in order to dismantle one's self. Otherwise, the unwary Westerner might misappropriate the principles of Buddhism, erroneously thinking that because there is no self, there must be no problem, errantly believing that they, after all, have no "problems," misguidedly thinking that they cannot have problems because there is no self.

Erich Fromm:

Summation:

Drop one's ego (63). 'Buddha nature' is in all of us (69).

Personal Takeaways:

We each have Buddha nature, meaning enlightened being, awakened one. If only we will awaken the Buddha nature within, acknowledging that each of us has the capacity of a Buddha, then we would be enlightened, in degrees, gradually.

John Welwood:

Summation:

Emotions seemingly move us beyond our control (79). Befriending emotions, rather than reacting against one's emotions (88), is what is required.

Personal Takeaways:

In Buddhism, emotions are not to be shunned but seen through; not ignored but owned up to. Seeing the transitory nature of our emotions is key to moving through our emotions.

Roger Welsh:

Summation:

Buddhism employs the 'don't know' mind (103), a humble admittance to the epistemological limits of human understanding. Additionally, resistance to fear/anxiety induces fear/anxiety (109). Therefore, don't identify self with one's moods (116).

Personal Takeaways:

From a Buddhistic perspective, it is vitally important not to attach to our moods; rather, just let moods and emotions pass through, like the proverbial 'clouds in the sky.' We are not our moods or emotions.

Chogyam Trungpa:

Summation:

Life is impermanence, transitoriness (127). And therapy is like hermeneutical clarifying (136).

Personal Takeaways:

Life is anicca, impermanence, so one must live without attachments; otherwise, one will become severely and continuously disappointed that they can't find any absolutes to desperately hold onto. Now, therapeutically speaking, one needs to cut through maya, as if one were clarifying life's situations in an interpretive manner.

John Welwood:

Summation:

Existential world collapse, groundlessness (148), is the phenomenon that takes place when one discovers that there is, after all, no ground to stand on. In this way, Buddhism goes further than existentialism by embracing non-solidity (151). Buddhism embraces non-solidity fully, not revolting against void, emptiness (152).

Personal Takeaways:

My long-standing affinities for the Western philosophical school of existentialism and phenomenology is a given, and so it makes me think I just might have an inside track to certain Buddhist principles, such as impermanence and suffering. My worldviews have always had an ultimate collapse and deflation about them. I have experienced a groundlessness that follows my worldview wherever I go. In the case of my 'Buddhistic existentialism,' I think that it is true that the existential ground of being, or Being, entail an ephemeral experience of a world in collapse, my being left with an utter despair that the ground underneath me is not there, after all. I concur that Buddhism goes further into this void of groundlessness than does existentialism; Buddhism bypasses the existential despair of non-being, obviating the need to posture the embodiment of existential revolt. Instead, Buddhism wholeheartedly embraces non-solidity, emptiness, dependent arising.

Book 7) *How To See Yourself as You Really Are* ~ **The 14th Dalai Lama (Tenzin Gyatso)**

Summation:

This work by the Dalai Lama has become a capstone to my innumerable years of studying Zen Buddhism. His work, written with demonstrative clarity, crystalizes for me the Buddhistic principles that I have been studying and imbibing from the previous Buddhist authors I have read. I have here included my own italicized captions – Meditation; Suffering; Love, Acceptance; and Emptiness, Impermanence – to help the reader to ascertain the Dalai Lama's thoughts in this work.

Meditation:

Meditation is essential to the process of awakening. Mindfulness is a form of introspection (106). And analytical meditation is a kind of focusing (87-88). Everything depends on mind as the authorizer (195-96).

Suffering:

The Dalai Lama addresses the origin of suffering – ignorance and greed – by isolating the factors that play a part in the manifestation of suffering. Ignorance mistakes objects (43) whereby mistaken beliefs superimpose onto objects, such as beauty/ugliness (45). And it is attachment that begats samsara, the cyclic existence (35) of birth, death, and rebirth.

Love, Acceptance:

Buddhism provides a space to cultivate love and acceptance towards all other sentient beings, not allowing harmful emotions to arise. Altruism towards all others (231) is vital to all world religions, which espouse love and a disciplined mind (14). Selflessness stops samsara's cyclical existence (41). Afflictive emotions obscure reality (53), such that karma – the law of cause and effect, physically and psychically – catches up with us, all the while inflicting pain and suffering. Karma is the agent of our actions (143). In light of this, our purpose is to be liberated from cyclic existence (29).

Emptiness, Impermanence:

The physical and psychical nature of the human condition can be addressed head-on with the dynamics of Buddhism's notion of "emptiness." For Buddhism, the defining nature of life can be expressed as anicca, which means impermanence, transitoriness, the everchanging condition of being human. And acceptance of our fate is best handled through the practice of wu-wei, which means non-doing and letting be, with effortless effort.

All phenomena are dependent-arisings, there is no inherent existence (60-61). Dependent-arisings can be found by looking at a table, which is, after all, a collection of parts – wood, legs, tabletop, bolts – such that the "table" does not exist in its own right (62). We are empty of inherent existence because phenomena are dependent-arisings (68-69), emptiness is empty of inherency (81). But to the Buddhist mentality, this emptiness is not an utter void (75), not utterly nonexistent (176-77), not anything like the Western notion of a scary nothingness and cynical nihilism.

In light of viewing life as dependent arisings, the 'I' (just like the table example) is not found, there is no solid 'I' (133), only a non-inherently existent 'I' (143). But the 'I' definitely exists, but in the sense of phenomena, dependent-arisings (63-66). Phenomena does not exist in its own right (188), but phenomena is always 'in relation to' (193), relative to. Truly, this is the stuff of particle physics (217).

Personal Takeaways:

The Dalai Lama touches upon the origin of suffering – ignorance and greed – which is remedied by love and acceptance; selflessness and compassion towards samsara's cyclical existence (cyclic existence – birth, death, and rebirth). And "mu" (nothing, empty) points to anicca (impermanence). The fact of the matter is that 'I' only exists as a non-inherently existent 'I,' an 'I' that is conventionally, but not ultimately, true. There is no inherent existence, only non-inherently so. For, we are, as the Dalai Lama states, "dependent arisings," no inherent existence.

Conclusion

I have lived most of my life aspiring to become what existentialist philosopher C.D. Keyes refers to as a "poetic nihilist;" this, in contradistinction to a "cynic nihilist." *God or Ichabod? A Nonviolent Christian Nihilism*, written by C.D. Keyes, delves deeply into these concepts. For Keyes, the lifeboat is sinking, and we are all on it, together, yet alone. The cynic nihilist, in response to the sinking boat of life, commences – out of anger and despair – to punch more holes in the bottom of the boat; while the poetic nihilist responds to the human situation by composing a song or a poem; all while the lifeboat is inevitably sinking. (If memory serves, I believe the orchestra aboard the Titanic went down whilst they played music.) There are choices: Bitterly and angrily respond with 'fear and loathing,' playing the role of the cynic nihilist, a destroyer; abhorring the human predicament; or, to respond graciously as the poetic nihilist, generating a therapeutic balm for the rest of humanity. As the Zen master says to the angry, disgruntled kid regarding his destructive behavior toward the human predicament, "You spit, I bow."

I hasten to add, in accordance with Nietzsche's eloquent statement from his *Birth of Tragedy*: "It is only as an aesthetic phenomenon that existence and the world are eternally justified." It is artistic expression and aesthetic appreciation, not religion, that allows one to hope and cope alongside the ultimate demise of the human condition. In Buddhistic terms, art, as well as any other human endeavor, reflects the transiency, impermanence, and ambiguity of existence.

Musical Interlude:

> My analyst told me that I was right out of my head, but I said, "Dear doctor I think that it's you instead. Because I, I got a thing that's unique and new, to prove it, I'll have the last laugh on you, 'cause instead of one head I got two. And you know two heads are better than one.

("Twisted," Joni Mitchell vocals, off her album *Court and Spark*; lyrics by Annie Ross)

In one of the Zen books that I have since lost, the author somewhere says something like, 'take life with utter seriousness, but also with a sense of humor, as a cosmic joke' (in a good way).

"Miracle, coincidence, or synchronicity?

You make the call!"

It is left to us to take the "leap," to "make the call;" not in some subjectivistic, solipsistic manner, mind you, but we must remember that the "observer" in us is always a part of the bigger picture of interpretation, of understanding reality or existence. Our making the call is especially crucial in situations that demand an ethical response. Life's situations happen to demand our making split-second decisions, decisions with incalculable significance, of ethical import. I am here thinking of Kierkegaard's appraisal of the human situation, that we must all make "leaps." I'm also reminded of the philosophical school of nominalism, where nominalism asserts that we 'name' the things we call reality; and whereby reality begats words which begat reality which begats words, ad infinitum.

But "words" have loosened their grip on me; words no longer (well, maybe this is not completely accurate) seem so suspicious. For, life is not a suspect any longer. Gradually, I have dropped the incriminating mind, no longer stoking the flames of an "existential gripe" with life, no longer the need to be troubled by the facts of life, no more accusatory "why." But the non-accusatory "why" is still with me, just not hauntingly so.

Finally, I shall close this work with a couple of amusing, thought-provoking Zen stories, and one personal anecdote.

A well-known Zen story:

Two monks walk a path to a nearby river. A woman asks for help getting across the river. One monk carries her across and sets her down on the other side. As the two monks resumed walking down the path, after some period had passed, the one monk said to the other, Don't you know, monks are not supposed to touch an unclean woman. The other monk replied, Are you still carrying that woman?!

A Zen Comic strip:

A disgruntled passerby snarls at the world in front of a Buddhist monk, and barks out, "What are you looking at?!" And the monk simply replies, "You spit, I bow."

A personal anecdote:

I leave the reader with this, the earlier referenced multipurposed saying of mine, "We all get there."

Made in the USA
Las Vegas, NV
15 August 2023

76138984R00085